OUR SOLAR SYSTEM

Black Holes

BY DANA MEACHEN RAU

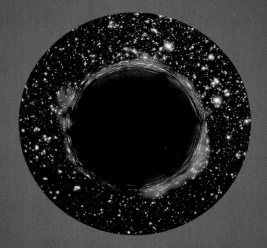

Content Adviser: Dr. Stanley P. Jones, Assistant Director, Washington, D.C., Operations, NASA-Sponsored Classroom of the Future

Science Adviser: Terrence E. Young Jr., M.Ed., M.L.S., Jefferson Parish (Louisiana) Public School System

Reading Adviser: Susan Kesselring, M.A., Literacy Educator, Rosemount-Apple Valley-Eagan (Minnesota) School District

COMPASS POINT BOOKS
MINNEAPOLIS, MINNESOTA

For Charlie and Allison—D.M.R

Compass Point Books
3109 West 50th Street, #115
Minneapolis, MN 55410

Visit Compass Point Books on the Internet at *www.compasspointbooks.com*
or e-mail your request to *custserv@compasspointbooks.com*

Photographs ©: NASA/G. Bacon/STScI, cover, 1, 4–5; ESA/NASA/Felix Mirabel (the French Atomic Energy
Commission & the Institute for Astronomy and Space Physics/Conicet of Argentina), 3, 24–25; NASA, 7, 28 (top);
PhotoDisc, 8–9 (all); Daniel Hodges, 10–11, 15 (right); NASA/CXC/M.Weiss, 13, 26 (left); NASA/CXC/MIT/F.T.
Baganoff, 17 (left); Aaron Horowitz/Corbis, 17 (right); Hulton/Archive by Getty Images, 19; Lisa Larsen/Time Life
Pictures/Getty Images, 20; Bettmann/Corbis, 21; Alistair Watters, 22–23; ESA-Ducros, 26–27; Comstock, 28–29.

Editor: Nadia Higgins
Lead Designer/Page production: The Design Lab
Photo researcher: Svetlana Zhurkina
Educational Consultant: Diane Smolinski

Managing Editor: Catherine Neitge
Art Director: Keith Griffin
Production Director: Keith McCormick
Creative Director: Terri Foley

Library of Congress Cataloging-in-Publication Data
Rau, Dana Meachen, 1971–
 Black holes / by Dana Meachen Rau.
   p. cm. — (Our solar system)
Includes index.
ISBN 0-7565-0849-5 (hardcover)
1. Black holes (Astronomy)—Juvenile literature. I. Title.
 QB843.B55R38 2005
 523.8'875—dc22   2004015567

Table of Contents

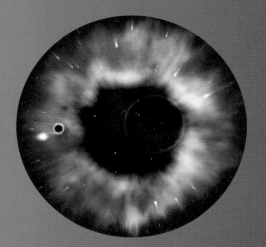

Invisible Spots in Outer Space

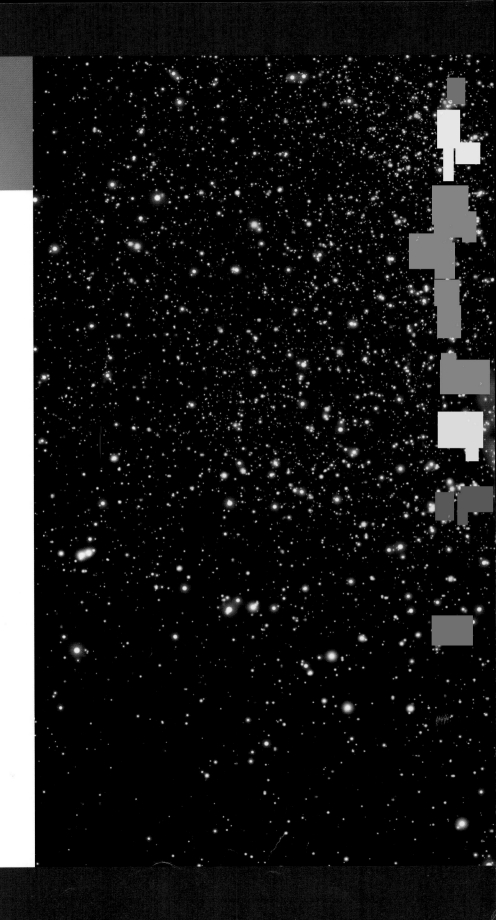

✦ Imagine trying to study something billions of miles away. Astronomers do that every day when they study the stars and planets. Now imagine trying to study something billions of miles away that is also invisible! That is what astronomers who study black holes have to do.

A black hole is one of the most mysterious objects in the universe. It is made up of a very dense object surrounded by an area of space. Anything that falls into the area is trapped—even light.

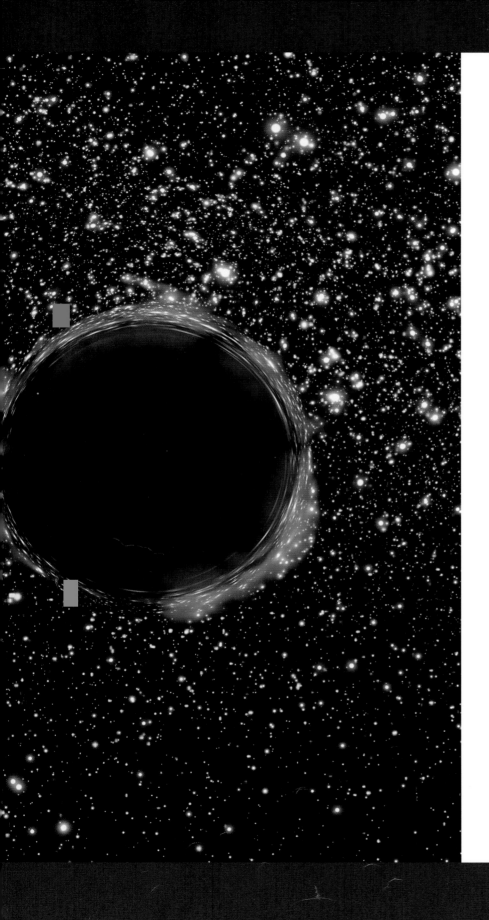

That makes black holes very difficult to study. Scientists can't actually see black holes, even with telescopes, because black holes are so dark. Scientists can't send up equipment to get close to them, either, because the equipment would be ruined. Even so, scientists still know a lot about black holes.

◄ *An artist's view of a black hole*

Three things help scientists understand black holes—gravity, escape velocity, and the speed of light. Gravity is a force that pulls objects toward a center point. Earth's gravity is what makes a ball fall to the ground and not float in the air. The sun has gravity, too, which pulls on Earth and the other planets in our solar system. Gravity makes the planets orbit, or travel around, the sun instead of moving off in different directions in space.

It is very hard to break the pull of a planet's gravity.

If something is fast enough, though, it can escape this strong force. For example, when a rocket launches, it travels so fast that it is able to escape the pull of Earth's gravity and travel into outer space. How fast the rocket needs to go is called its escape velocity.

The speed of light is the third idea needed to understand black holes. It might be strange to think of light as having a speed. You flip a switch, and light seems to instantly fill the

A rocket must travel 7 miles (11.2 kilometers) ▶
in one second to launch into space.

room. However, it really takes a tiny amount of time for light to travel from a lamp to your eyes. Then you can see objects. Nothing in the entire universe travels faster than light. Light rays travel at 186,282 miles (298,051 kilometers) per second. That's about 10 million times faster than a car on the highway!

So how do these three things—gravity, escape velocity, and the speed of light—explain black holes? A black hole has incredibly strong gravity. The gravity is so strong that it pulls in

It takes about eight minutes for light ▸
from the sun to travel to Earth.

anything that gets too close. Nothing has an escape velocity high enough to avoid it. Not even light, the fastest thing in the universe, travels fast enough to get out. Since no light comes out of a black hole, we cannot see a black hole.

▲ *Gravity, the force that causes a black hole to form, is the same force that causes a ball to drop. However, a black hole's gravity is much, much stronger than gravity on Earth.*

If You Could Visit a Black Hole

✦ Imagine that you and three friends are each holding the corner of a blanket. Then you roll a bowling ball into the center of the blanket. Even if you and your friends hold the blanket tightly, the ball will make the center of the blanket sag. The ball is bending the blanket.

This is like what happens to space around a black hole. Space is like the blanket, and the black hole is like the bowling ball. Space bends around the black hole's heavy center.

Space bends around a black hole the way ▸ *the blanket bends around this bowling ball.*

A black hole isn't really a hole. It is more like a funnel with a tiny ball in the bottom. The funnel is like the blanket. It is the space that the ball has bent. The outer edge of the funnel is called the event horizon. The ball, at the narrow bottom of the funnel, is called the singularity. If an object is outside of the event horizon, it is safe. It is outside the range of a black hole's pull. However, once something passes the horizon's edge, it falls down to the singularity and can never get out.

You could never visit a black hole, but think about

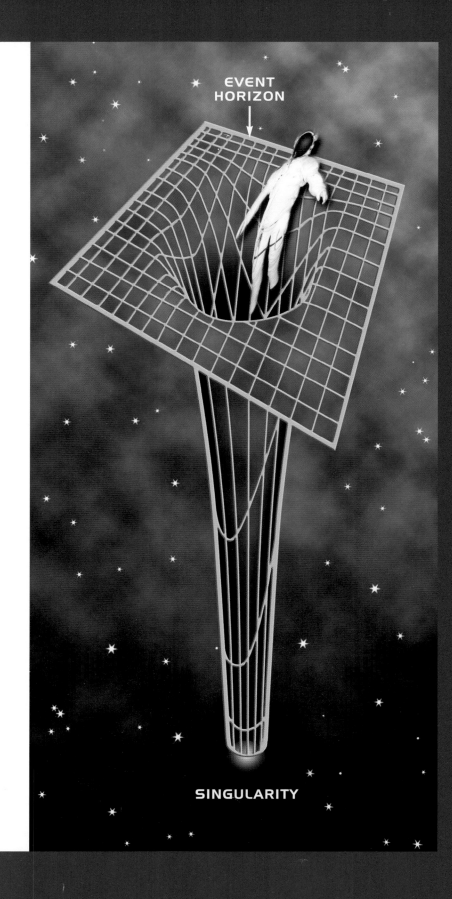

EVENT HORIZON

SINGULARITY

what would happen to you if you could. As you neared the event horizon, you would feel the pull of the black hole's strong gravity. If you approached feet first, the pull of gravity on your feet would be stronger than the gravity on your head. The difference between these two forces would stretch out your body until it was long and thin, like a rubber band.

Once your body passed the event horizon, you would be sucked in. In a few seconds, you would circle down to the singularity, like water going down a drain. You would never be able to get out again.

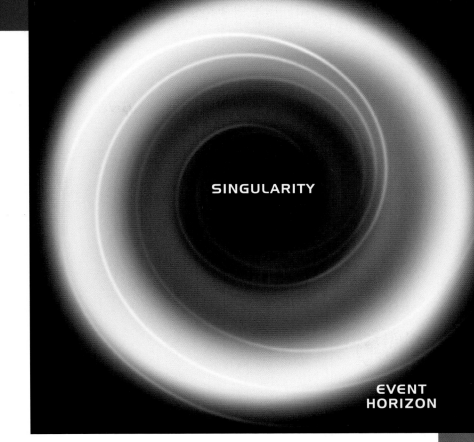

SINGULARITY

EVENT HORIZON

Because the black hole's gravity is so incredibly strong, the only way out would be if you could reach an escape velocity faster than the speed of light. Since light is the fastest thing in the universe, this would be impossible.

▲ *An artist's view of the top of a black hole*

How Black Holes Are Formed

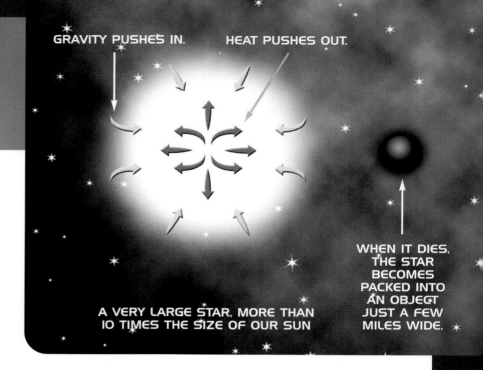

GRAVITY PUSHES IN.   HEAT PUSHES OUT.

A VERY LARGE STAR, MORE THAN 10 TIMES THE SIZE OF OUR SUN

WHEN IT DIES, THE STAR BECOMES PACKED INTO AN OBJECT JUST A FEW MILES WIDE.

Stars burn for billions of years, and then they die. Most black holes are dead stars.

What makes a star die? The inside of a star is filled with a gas called hydrogen. The hydrogen in a star is always burning. This burning gives off a lot of heat. The heat moves outward from the inside of the star. At the same time, gravity is pushing in on the star. The heat pushes out, and the gravity pushes in. This balance makes the star keep its shape.

Much as a fire in a fireplace needs wood to burn, the fire inside a star always needs hydrogen to keep going. However, the hydrogen does not last forever. After billions of years, the hydrogen in a star is all burned up. That is when a star dies.

There is no longer heat pushing out of the star, but gravity is still pushing in. The star caves in on itself. It becomes incredibly heavy and dense. A very large star, one that is more than

THE DEAD STAR'S GRAVITY IS SO STRONG,
IT BECOMES A BLACK HOLE.

10 times the size of our sun, gets smaller and smaller and denser and denser until it is only a few miles wide. Almost all the material that made up the large star is now packed into a tiny space. This makes the gravity of the condensed star much stronger. Its gravity becomes so strong that it turns into a black hole. It will pull in anything that gets near it.

Density has to do with how much something weighs compared to how big it is. Imagine two balls that weigh the same. One is a beach ball and one is a marble. The marble is much denser than the beach ball because it is more compact.

Monster Black Holes

Black holes that are formed when stars die are called stellar black holes. Scientists believe there may be "supermassive" black holes as well. These black holes are so powerful that scientists also call them monster black holes.

Scientists came up with the idea of supermassive black holes by watching how stars move within a galaxy. Scientists noticed that stars seem to circle the center of a galaxy, much like the way the planets orbit the sun. That meant there would have to be an object creating strong gravity at the galaxy's center. This object, which was pulling on the stars, could be a black hole.

Such a black hole would have to be very large, or supermassive. These huge black holes were probably created when stars in the center of a galaxy

Scientists believe there is a black hole at the center of our galaxy, the Milky Way. Discovered in January 2000, this black hole has been called Sagittarius A* (pronounced A-star).

died. The dead stars turned into stellar black holes. Then they may have sucked each other in to form one huge black hole.

Scientists now believe that most galaxies have black holes

▲ *In this illustration, stars circle around a black hole at the center of a galaxy.*

◀ *The presence of energy in the form of X-rays can be a sign of a nearby black hole. An X-ray telescope took this image of energy around the monster black hole believed to be at the center of our galaxy.*

at their centers. Around these centers, scientists have noticed lots of orbiting stars and gases. These stars and gases orbit so fast that they give off energy, which can be detected by special telescopes. Only a supermassive black hole could create that much energy.

Some people have made up fantastical stories about black holes. They even believe that two black holes end to end, called a wormhole, would make time travel possible.

Ideas About Black Holes

✦ If black holes are impossible to see, then how did people discover them? Black holes began in the imaginations of scientists. Before they knew if black holes were even possible, people developed theories about space objects with strong gravity.

The study of these types of objects began in the late 1700s. A Frenchman named Pierre LaPlace (1749–1827) used math to try to explain black holes. LaPlace developed the idea that the denser

◀ *The French thinker Pierre LaPlace developed the first theories about black holes.*

an object is, the stronger its gravity. The stronger the gravity, the faster the escape velocity that is needed to break away from its pull.

Other scientists after him used math to figure out how a very dense object would affect space around it. They theorized about objects so dense that not even light could escape. It was not until the 1930s that scientists began to think such objects could actually exist. They developed ideas about a point of strong gravity (the singularity) with a funnel-shaped area (the event horizon) around it. They connected this idea to dying stars.

Then, in 1969, black holes got their name. The American scientist John Archibald Wheeler (1911–) decided "black hole" would be the best name for something so dark it made objects near it disappear.

Today, Stephen Hawking (1942–), an English scientist, is one of the most famous people thinking about black holes. In his popular books, he has used his ideas about black holes to help explain how the universe came to be.

◄◄ *The American scientist John Archibald Wheeler came up with the term* black hole.

◄ *The English scientist Stephen Hawking is a leader in the study of black holes today.*

Studying Black Holes Today

Even though black holes are invisible, scientists can still study them. Using several different kinds of telescopes, scientists observe the areas around black holes. They see how a black hole affects the things around it. The best way scientists can study black holes is by looking at binary stars. Binary stars are two stars that orbit each other.

If scientists see a star orbiting what looks like an empty space, they guess that there might be a black hole

An artist's illustration of binary stars ▶

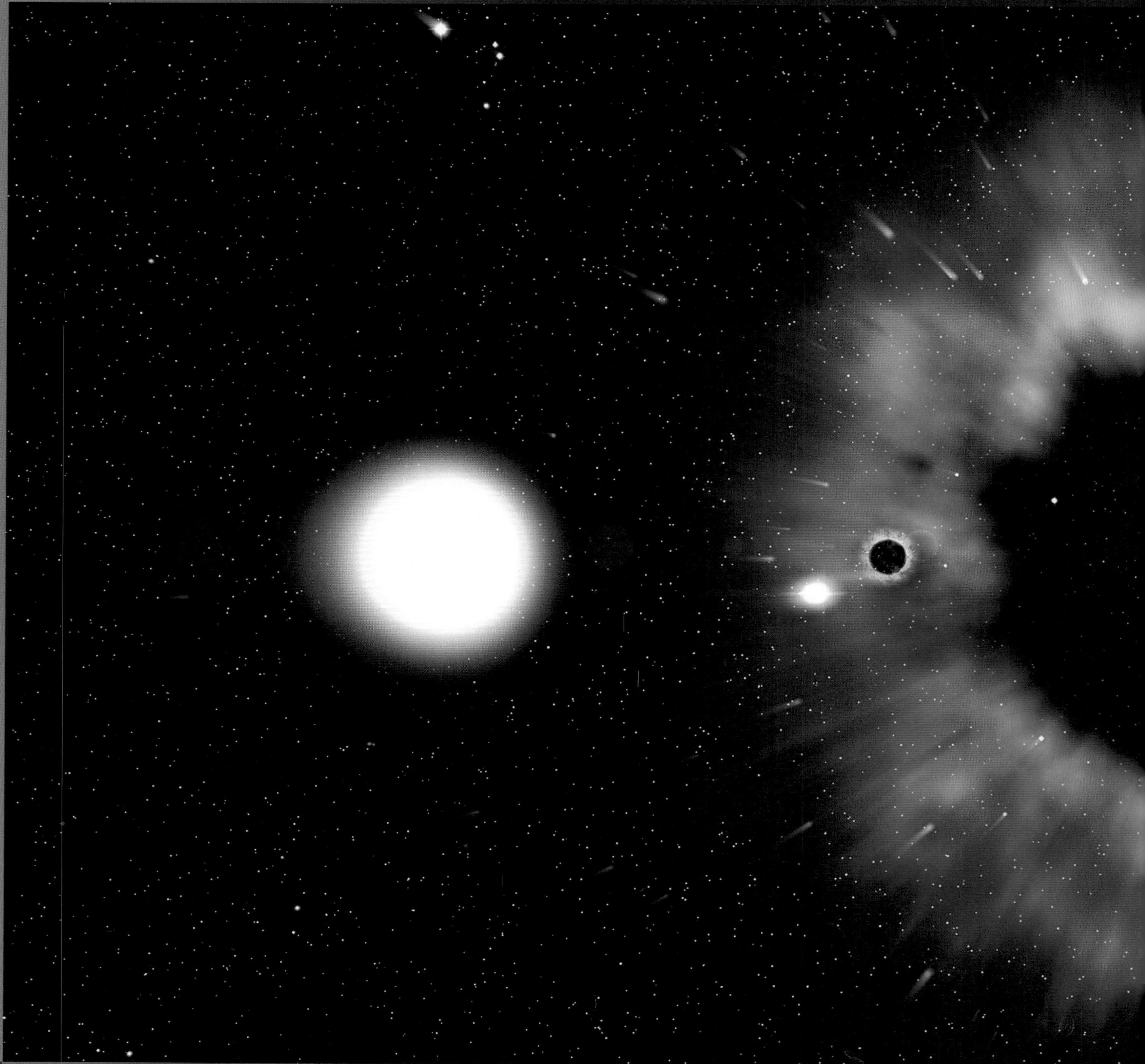

there. The black hole may have once been one of the stars in the pair. Since a black hole has strong gravity, it might pull some of the gases off of the star next to it. When this happens, the gases get very hot. They give off energy in the form of X-rays. Scientists can read these X-rays with special telescopes.

In February 2004, astronomers were thrilled to detect X-rays from the distant galaxy RX J1242-11. They believe the X-rays might have been the result of a very powerful black hole shredding

◄ *In this illustration, a star orbits a black hole. The black hole may have once been a binary star.*

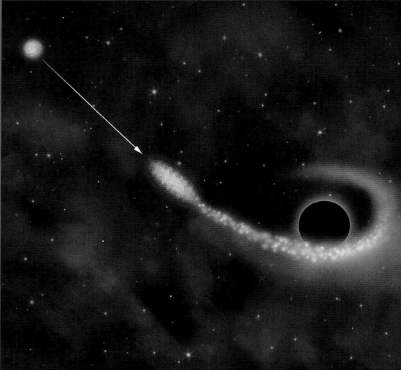

a nearby star to pieces.
Exciting discoveries like this
will always keep us looking
to the skies to find out more
about these mysterious
black holes.

*As a star gets sucked toward a black hole, ▲
it is stretched apart. Hot gases from the
star give off a blast of X-rays, which are
picked up by X-ray telescopes.*

*This X-ray telescope, called the ▶
XMM-Newton, looks for activity in
space where scientists believe black
holes may be hiding.*

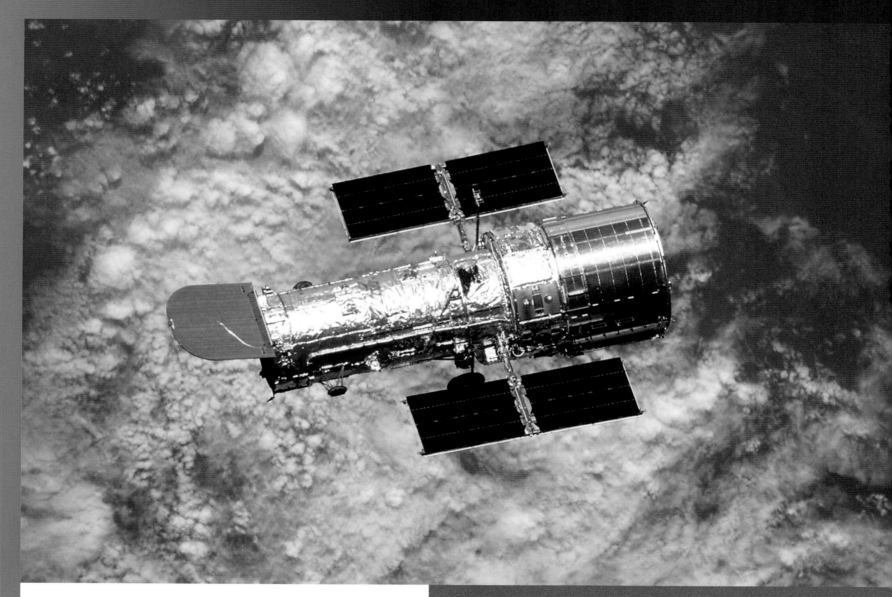

The Hubble Space Telescope takes ▲
photos of deep space. It also has special
equipment that can tell how fast stars
and gases are swirling around what
might be black holes.

Radio telescopes on Earth pick up ▶
radio signals from outer space that offer
clues about black holes.

Glossary

binary—having to do with two things

dense—heavy for its size; compact

escape velocity—how fast an object has to go to break out of a specific area of gravity

galaxy—a group of billions of stars that travel together through space

singularity—the bottom of a black hole; most of the material that once made up a star condensed into an incredibly dense object

stellar—having to do with stars

telescope—a tool used by astronomers to see or collect information about distant objects

theories—ideas about how or why something came to be

X-ray—a strong, invisible beam of energy that can be detected by special telescopes

Did You Know?

- Our sun is a star that would never become a black hole. It is too small.

- In July 2004, scientist Stephen Hawking presented a surprising new theory. Like most scientists, Hawking believed that black holes destroyed everything they came into contact with. Now he believes black holes may eventually spit out pieces of objects they've swallowed—though the pieces wouldn't look at all like they did before.

- A black hole's size depends on how big the star was that created it. The smallest ones, from stars about 10 times the size of our sun, would create a black hole about 19 miles (30.4 km) from one end of the event horizon to the other. But a very large star, one that started out 100 million times the size of our sun, would create a black hole about 2 million miles (3.2 million km) wide.

- In the 1970s, scientists discovered the galaxy Cygnus X-1. It gave off a lot of X-rays. This was one of the first galaxies they felt very sure contained a black hole.

Want to Know More?

AT THE LIBRARY

Ford, Harry. *The Young Astronomer.* New York: Dorling Kindersley, 1998.

Gifford, Clive. *The Kingfisher Facts and Records Book of Space.* New York: Kingfisher, 2001.

Mitton, Jacqueline, and Simon Mitton. *Scholastic Encyclopedia of Space.* New York: Scholastic, 1999.

Vogt, Gregory L. *Deep Space Astronomy.* Brookfield, Conn.: Twenty-First Century Books, 1999.

ON THE WEB

For more information on **black holes,** use FactHound to track down Web sites related to this book.

1. Go to *www.facthound.com*
2. Type in a search word related to this book or this book ID: **0756508495**.
3. Click on the *Fetch It* button.

Your trusty FactHound will fetch the best Web sites for you!

ON THE ROAD

Adler Planetarium and Astronomy Museum
1300 S. Lake Shore Drive
Chicago, IL 60605-2403
312/922-STAR
To visit the oldest planetarium in the Western Hemisphere

National Air and Space Museum
Sixth and Independence Avenue Southwest
Washington, DC 20560
202/357-2700
To learn more about the solar system and space exploration

National Radio Astronomy Observatory
The Very Large Array
P.O. Box O
1003 Lopezville Road
Socorro, NM 87801-0387
505/835-7000
To see a collection of 27 radio antennae that are always collecting the energy coming from deep space

Mount Wilson Observatory
Mount Wilson, CA 91023
626/793-3100
To see the telescope that many famous astronomers have used to study the night sky

Index

◄ **About the Author:** *Dana Meachen Rau loves to study space. Her office walls are covered with pictures of planets, astronauts, and spacecraft. She also likes to look up at the sky with her telescope and write poems about what she sees. Ms. Rau is the author of more than 100 books for children, including nonfiction, biographies, storybooks, and early readers. She lives in Burlington, Connecticut, with her husband, Chris, and children, Charlie and Allison.*